Clement
5/6/92

$12.95

D0556941

Programming with curses

John Strang

O'Reilly & Associates, Inc.
103 Morris Street
Sebastopol, CA 95472

Programming with curses
by John Strang

Editor: Tim O'Reilly

Copyright © 1991 O'Reilly & Associates, Inc.
All rights reserved.

Printed in the United States of America

Many of the designations used by manufacturers and sellers to distinguish their products are claimed as trademarks. Where those designations appear in this book, and O'Reilly and Associates, Inc. was aware of a trademark claim, the designations have been printed in caps or initial caps.

While every precaution has been taken in the preparation of this book, the publisher takes no responsibility for errors or omissions, or for damages resulting from the use of the information herein.

Please address comments and questions in care of the publisher:

O'Reilly & Associates, Inc.
103 Morris Street
Sebastopol, CA 95472
800-338-6887
international +1-707-829-0515

UUCP: uunet!ora!nuts
Internet: nuts@ora.uu.com

[10/91]

TABLE OF CONTENTS

Quick Reference

Preface

A Library for Screen Manipulation

curses is the UNIX library of functions for controlling a terminal's video display screen from a C program. *curses* can be used to provide a screen driver for a program (such as a visual editor) or to improve a program's user interface. This library supplies the C programmer with optimized cursor motion, physical terminal independence, multiple windows, and video attributes.

As a C programmer, you need to know about *curses* and how to use it. What is most important in understanding *curses* is examining its basic data structure called a WINDOW. You will learn what a WINDOW is, and how *curses* functions manipulate it.

You will also learn about the UNIX facilities that make it possible to write a program regardless of what type of terminal it is going to be run on.

Once you understand this background material, you are ready to learn the individual functions in the *curses* library. You want to know how to use them in a program and test your understanding by looking at examples of code.

Scope of this Handbook

The purpose of this handbook is to help you make use of the *curses* library in your C programs. We think we have done more than simply describe the individual functions in the library. We have tried to present ample material on *curses* and its implementation in UNIX so that you understand the whole as well as its parts.

The author of *curses* is Ken Arnold who wrote the package while at Berkeley. His article entitled "*Screen Updating and Cursor Movement Optimization: A Library Package*" is the source for information about *curses*. Mark Horton at Bell Laboratories, author of *terminfo*, wrote a second version of *curses* that retained all of our Arnold's functions and added others to take advantage of *terminfo* features. Now distributed with AT&T System V Release 2, Horton's package is sometimes called AT&T *curses*. Arnold's original package, sometimes called *Berkeley curses*, (one system we know of has *bcurses* and *curses*) is the one we cover in this handbook.

Chapter 1 describes the use of windows in *curses*. It covers the representation of the terminal screen as a C data structure and how windows are created and displayed.

Chapter 2 describes how facilities provided by the UNIX operating system allow terminal-independent applications to be written with *curses*. It also describes the contents of the *<curses.h>* header file.

Chapter 3 describes each of the functions in the *curses* library. The functions are organized into related groups, and examples from a sample program are used to demonstrate many of the functions. The chapter also describes how to compile and link a program that uses *curses*.

The *curses* library functions are listed in a quick reference at the end of this handbook.

1
Understanding Windows

Introduction

Two great programs of the last decade are the visual editor and *visicalc*. Both do what could be done before. Visual editors do what could be done with a line editor. *visicalc*, and the many spreadsheet programs that followed, do what accounting programs had long done. They are still great programs. They are great because they use the whole screen to display their information in an attractive, organized, relevant style that outshines their line-oriented predecessors. It is a simple and enormous difference.

Every program benefits from a good display. If the application is right, as it was for visual editors and *visicalc*, it can make the program great. Why then, do so many programs limit themselves to sequential, line-oriented output at the bottom of the screen? Because it is easy. This is not to criticize programmers, who must put their effort where it is most productive. It is to ask: why isn't there an easy way to write programs that use the whole screen? Why isn't there a library of compiled procedures that do the work of managing the whole screen? Well, there is: *curses*.

curses is a package of functions in the UNIX library for use in C programs. Your compiled and linked code can be ported because *curses* is terminal-independent. Among the functions to be found in *curses* are those that:

- Move the cursor to any point on the screen

- Insert text anywhere on the screen, doing it even in highlight mode

- Divide the screen into rectangular areas called windows

- Manage each window independently, so you can be scrolling one window while erasing a line in another

- Draw a box around a window using a character of your choice

If these features leave you unimpressed, remember that they are only tools. When you use these tools in your program, the results can be spectacular. The point is — *curses* is easy to use and ready to go — so that you can concentrate on what you want your program to do. *curses* will make your program look sharp.

Windows, Screens and Images

Conceptually, a window is an independent rectangular area of characters displayed on the screen. Physically, a window is a WINDOW, that is, a C data structure that holds all the information about a window. Understanding windows as a concept and as a physical structure is important to using *curses*.

The Standard Screen - *stdscr*

stdscr refers to the "standard screen". The traditional definition of the "standard screen" is a window or a set of windows that fills the entire screen of a video display terminal.

That definition has little practical value, however, because "screen" has come to mean the physical terminal screen. If the screen is what you can touch, then "*stdscr*" refers to what you can see on your screen. *stdscr* represents the window or windows that fill up the entire screen.

The structure that describes *stdscr* is a WINDOW, or more precisely, a pointer to a WINDOW. A WINDOW is a character array that maintains an image of the terminal screen, known as the **screen image**.

The screen image array in *stdscr* is automatically made the length and width of the terminal screen. Thus, there is one character in that array for every place on the screen. A useful analogy is that of a bit-mapped terminal, which contains an area of memory in which each bit corresponds to a pixel on the screen. That bit-mapped memory and the character array in *stdscr* are images of the physical screen.

Adding Characters

Initially, the screen image is filled with blanks. As you use *curses*, you will put characters in that array. This is just the same as turning bits on and off in the bit-mapped memory. There are *curses* functions for putting characters into the array. Some of these functions, which are cousins of the familiar C I/O routines, are:

> **insch()**
>
> **addch()**
>
> **addstr()**
>
> **printw()**

Many of the functions in *curses* are just different ways to put characters on the screen.

Moving the Logical Cursor

Normal terminal I/O is sequential. A cursor marks the location where the next character will be printed.

The purpose of windows is to provide for non-sequential I/O. To do this, *curses* employs a **logical cursor** instead of a physical cursor. A logical cursor is a (y,x) marker in each window.

"Logical" describes a concept applied to a window, while "physical" applies to the terminal itself. The coordinates *y* and *x* mark the position of the logical cursor anywhere inside the window's screen image.

The **move(y,x)** command is used to specify a position for the logical cursor prior to inserting or deleting text with the next command.

Refreshing the Screen

After you have inserted characters into the character array, you are ready to display the character array on the screen. This is called refreshing the screen.

On a bit-mapped terminal, the refresh is automatic. Every time the electron gun sweeps the screen, the current contents of the bit-mapped image are displayed.

Not so with *curses*. The screen is only refreshed when you give the command **refresh()**. What is lost in instant feedback is gained in efficiency. You can make a number of changes to the window, then have them all displayed at once. **refresh()** calculates the optimal way to change the physical screen so it looks like the current window.

To summarize, when you work with a window, you follow this procedure:

Initialize WINDOW to represent window on the screen,

| |

Insert and move characters in the character array,

| |

Refresh to display the updated window on the screen,

| |

Make more changes to the window,

| |

And refresh the screen again.

It is very important that you understand the **refresh()** algorithm. **refresh()** does not output the whole screen image: that would be inefficient at 9600 baud and painful at 1200 baud.

Instead, **refresh()** tries to minimize the number of characters it must output to the screen. It sends only the characters that have been changed since the last refresh, after first moving the physical cursor to those positions.

The Current Screen — *curscr*

curses does not know directly what the terminal is displaying; it would be even slower to have to query the terminal to find out what character is being displayed at each location. Instead, *curses* keeps an image of what it thinks the screen looks like in a window called *curscr*.

curscr, like *stdscr*, is created automatically when you initialize curses with **initscr()**. *curscr* is a WINDOW, and has a screen image the size of the physical screen. When **refresh()** is called, it writes the characters that it is sending to the terminal into their corresponding location in the screen image of *curscr*. *curscr* contains the image of the screen as *curses* thinks it was made to look by the last **refresh()**.

refresh() is the only function that changes the screen image of *curscr* (unless you specifically tell one to). Unless you have good reason, do not change the screen image of *curscr*. This way it will stay as **refresh()** expects it. You can work on *stdscr*, and create new windows and sub-windows as desired, but leave *curscr* alone.

refresh() uses the screen image in *curscr* to minimize its work. When it goes to refresh a window, it compares the contents of that window to *curscr*. **refresh()** assumes that the physical screen looks like *curscr* so it does not output characters that are the same in *curscr* and the window that is being refreshed. In this way, **refresh()** minimizes the number of characters that it sends to the screen and saves a great deal of time.

curses also keeps track of the first and last characters on each line of a window that were changed since the last **refresh()** of that window. (The _firstch and _lastch commands are discussed later in the section "The WINDOW Structure".) This also helps to reduce the number of characters that must be checked against *curscr*.

Some Potential Problems

curscr has practical value to you. First, knowing the **refresh()** mechanism allows you to understand how it can be confused (as described below) and thus avoid those situations. Second, *curscr* provides a cure when the screen does get garbled: issue the command **refresh(***curscr***)** and the screen will be returned to the way *curses* thought it looked at the previous **refresh()**.

Problems arise when *curscr* and the terminal screen do not match. You cannot mix windows with regular output functions such as **printf()** and **putchar()** because **refresh()** does not know what those output functions did or even that they were called. **refresh()** will blissfully write only the characters that have been changed in the screen image and are different from *curscr*. The mixture of output from windows and regular I/O can be horrible.

For the same reason, you must use the *curses* input functions such as **getch()** and **scanw()** and not the standard I/O input functions such as **getchar() and scanf()**.

The *curses* input functions can be set to echo or not echo input. If they are echoing input, they also store the input in the screen image of the given window. In that way, the screen image is updated along with the screen and inconsistencies are avoided. The screen image in *curscr* is not changed when you are echoing characters to another window but is left as it was at the last **refresh()**.

Problems can arise even when you use the *curses* input functions. For character input to work perfectly, the screen image in the windows must be exactly the same as the physical terminal screen. The physical cursor on the screen must be in the same position as the logical cursor in the screen image that is echoing the input. This avoids most problems, but not all.

Depending on what input mode you are in, certain input can cause problems. Some input characters may have control code effects on the terminal, or a tab may be handled differently in the screen image than on the screen. On some terminals, the screen image may be shorter than the screen, and when the input text goes off the right end, it scrolls to the next line in the screen image while continuing on the same line on the physical screen. Any character that misaligns the logical cursor from the physical cursor will cause problems.

Multiple Windows

You can do a lot of work using only the automatic window *stdscr*. Sometimes, however, *stdscr* is not enough and you will need to define windows in addition to *stdscr*.

You can create new windows in two ways:

1. Divide an existing window into sub-windows with **subwin()**.

2.　Define one or more new windows with **newwin()**.

Dividing an existing window into sub-windows permits you to manage the sub-windows independently. Then you can limit functions like text input, scrolling, wraparound, boxes, and refreshes to that single window. New windows can be defined that cover the same area of the screen as any existing window. You can make the screen display the old window and the new window at different times. Sub-windows and new windows, like *curscr* and *stdscr*, use the same WINDOW data structure.

There is a fundamental physical difference between sub-windows and new windows. It's a difference in the content of the WINDOW structure that is used to represent them.

Both sub-windows and new windows are WINDOWs. Therefore, both have all the fields that are in a WINDOW structure. The difference is that no new character array is created for a sub-window. Instead, it uses the part of the character array of its parent window that maps to the appropriate part of the screen. (The character array is physically stored in a WINDOW as char **y, so sub-windows just make **y point into the already-allocated array of the parent.)

This means that changes made to the character array of the sub-window will also be made in that part of the character array of the parent, and vice-versa. They are independent in every other way, with all the benefits of independence. Sharing the character array not only saves space, it can be used as a tool.

A new window, on the other hand, has its own independent character array created for it.

You can do a lot more with multiple windows, but it is also more confusing. It is easy to mangle the display when you use overlapping windows. Here is a brief list of things to think about when using multiple windows:

1. Consider how the screen is going to look when you are done.

2. Remember that each window is independent and has independent properties.

3. Remember that sub-windows use the same character array as their parent window.

4. Understand **refresh()** and *curscr*, because they are the only way one window can find out what another window has done.

The WINDOW Structure

The WINDOW structure is so basic to *curses* that it deserves a complete description. Understanding the WINDOW structure will help you learn and remember the *curses* commands. In fact, if some command seems strange or counter-intuitive to you, it is probably a result of the WINDOW structure.

In principle, a complete description of the WINDOW structure is impossible because *curses* is defined by the command set, not the implementation. Each new version of *curses* is free to redefine the WINDOW.

In practice, the structure we describe is almost universally used. A few extra flags or fields may be added, but the basis usually remains the same. To see the actual WINDOW structure used on your system, look in the *<curses.h>* header file (*/usr/include/curses.h*).

WINDOWS are usually implemented by the structure shown:

```
struct {
short _cury, _curx;
short _maxy, _maxx;
short _begy, _begx;
short _flags;
bool _clear;
bool _leave;
```

```
bool _scroll;
char **_y;
short *_firstch;
short *_lastch;
}
```

_cury and **_curx** describe the position of the logical cursor in the window. They contain the current (y,x) coordinates in the window for the next character to be inserted. They are listed here as (y,x) and not (x,y) because *curses* functions use them in that order. _curx and _cury are window-relative, not screen-relative. The upper left corner of the window is represented as (_cury, _curx) = (0,0), even if the window is located in the middle of the screen.

_maxx and **_maxy** are the height and width of the window. Thus, they are one more than the maximum values allowed for _curx and _cury (remember that _cury and _curx are zero based).

_begx and **_begy** are the position of the upper left corner of the window relative to the upper left corner of the screen. They thus fix the position of the entire window. (_begy, begx) = (0, 0) is the upper left corner of the screen.

_flags is a collection of bitflags. These flags tell about the window, and are mostly used by the **refresh()** function for optimization. Each bit is a different flag. The flags are, from least significant to most significant:

000001   _SUBWIN if the window is a sub-window.

000002   _ENDLINE if the right end of each line is the edge of the screen.

000004   _FULLWIN if the window fills the whole screen.

000010   _SCROLLWIN if the last character of the window is the lower right edge of the screen. The terminal should scroll if a character is put there.

000020   _FLUSH is reserved for use in future releases.

000040   _FULLINE if each line of the window reaches across the width of the screen.

000200   _STANDOUT if characters added to the screen should be added in standout mode.

000400   _INSL if a line has been inserted in this window.

001000   _DELL if a line has been deleted from this window.

_clear is set by clearok() and clear() if the screen should be cleared directly by using the terminal clear control code before doing the next refresh. refresh() will only issue this control code if the window occupies the entire screen (the _FULLWIN flag must be set) even if _clear is set. bool is defined in the <curses.h> header file, and is simply an integer which is used as a boolean value.

_leave tells refresh() to set (_curx, _cury) to the position of the cursor after the last character has been changed by refresh(). If _leave is not set, the cursor will be moved to the position of (_curx, _cury) after the reset is complete. Either way, the cursor and (curx, _cury) will align, _leave decides which is made to match the other. _leave is set by leaveok().

_scroll is set if scrolling is allowed for the window. _scroll is determined by the user (with the scrollok() function) and means logical scrolling within the window, not real scrolling done by the terminal. Logical scrolling will shift lines up and add a new blank line all within the window by manipulating the **y character array. Logical scrolling may be done to windows that are shorter than the screen and which do not reach the bottom line. _scroll is set by scrollok().

**_y is the pointer to the character array that contains the screen image. Because of the way C handles multi-dimensional arrays, **_y is a pointer to a list of pointers (a one-dimensional array) which each point to a list of characters. Each list of characters represents a line of the window. y[i] is the pointer to the ith line of the window and y[i][j] is the jth character on that line. This implementation makes moving a window difficult.

*_firstch is essential to the **refresh()** function. ***_firstch** is an array of numbers, with each number corresponding to a line in the window. The numbers in ***_firstch** are the locations of the leftmost character on that line that has been changed since the window was last refreshed. This allows **refresh()** to know that no characters to the left of *firstch[i]* have been changed on line *i*. The locations are relative to the window so they are measured from the left edge of the window, not the left edge of the terminal. If no character has been changed, the ***_firstch** entry is set to _NOCHANGE, which is defined as -1.

*_lastch is an array just like ***_firstch**. It tells **refresh()** which is the rightmost character changed since the last refresh, or it uses _NOCHANGE if the line is unchanged. **refresh()** knows that only the characters between ***_firstch** and ***_lastch** could have been changed. Like ***_firstch**, ***_lastch** is relative to the window, not to the screen.

2
Terminal Independence

Introduction

When you first look at what *curses* offers, the importance of terminal independence is likely to be overshadowed by the windowing features. In fact, terminal independence is the foundation of *curses*. If you were to write a package equivalent to *curses*, you would have as much trouble in making the package terminal-independent as you would in creating screen-handling features.

Terminal independence lets the programmer write programs that make use of the advanced features of intelligent terminals. Terminal independence means that a program can control the display screen of a **DEC vt100** or a **Wyse 50** or a hundred other new and old types of terminals. The best part for a programmer is that the program itself does not have to account for the variety of available terminals.

This chapter will briefly describe the UNIX facilities that make it possible to develop terminal-independent programs with *curses*. Throughout this chapter we will also be examining the contents of *<curses.h>*. This header file must be included in any program that uses *curses*. It contains definitions of datatypes, such as the WINDOW structure, and declares global variables.

What is Terminal Independence?

Any program, whether it makes use of *curses* or not, can print one character after another to the the screen. Every terminal prints the character 'A' when it is sent an 'A'. If a control code, such as "^A", is sent, however, one type of terminal might clear the screen while another might go into standout mode. A program needs to be able to send the proper control code to the terminal to get the appropriate result. Given that there are so many different types of terminals, you can see that it is difficult for a program to control the terminal screen.

UNIX contains a database that describes the control codes used by hundreds of terminals. Each make of terminal has an entry in the database and it is identified by the manufacturer's name and the product-line number. The entry lists the control codes used to access specific features or capabilities of the terminal.

The first UNIX database facility developed for dealing with the differences among terminals is called *termcap*. A second database facility has been introduced called *terminfo*. The implementation of *curses* is dependent upon either *termcap* or *terminfo*.

Termcap

/etc/termcap is a text file that contains the *termcap* database. Each entry in *termcap* is made up of:

> **Comment Lines** that begin with a sharp sign (#). Typically, a comment line describes the manufacturer of the terminal or the creator of the *termcap* entry.
>
> **Alias Names** that are used to identify the entry in the database. At the beginning of a UNIX session, a user sets the environment variable

"TERM" to the appropriate alias name that identifies his terminal.

List of Capabilities that describe the specific control codes for accessing the various features of a terminal. Each capability is identified by a two-letter symbol and is separated in the listing by a colon. There are boolean, string and numeric capabilities.

curses loads the terminal capabilities from */etc/termcap* into external variables declared in *<curses.h>*. The external variables all have names consisting of two capital letters (AM, BS, etc.) that correspond to the lower case names of the capabilities.

The **boolean type** declaration is used for Boolean capabilities, which do not have arguments. The boolean capability is included in the *termcap* entry to indicate that the feature exists. "bs" is a boolean capability that indicates whether or not a terminal has a backspace key. If it is defined in the *termcap* entry, then BS will be true.

The **char type** is used to declare variables that are pointers to the values of the string capabilities. For instance, the "do" capability contains the control code that moves the cursor down one line. Its value might be "^J" and is assigned to "*DO".

Generally, the programmer does not have to be concerned with the *termcap* database. *curses* takes care of all this for you and you don't need to be concerned with terminal capabilities. All of the variables are loaded at run-time so that the program can use whatever terminal is there.

However, for debugging purposes or reasons of efficiency, your code can access the variables as easily as the *curses* procedures can. You can use the terminal-specific data in these variables to build utilities to supplement *curses*. In fact, if all you are interested in are the terminal capabilities, you can use **initscr()** (or **setterm()** directly) to load specific variables. It is the easiest way to access */etc/termcap*.

Terminfo

The *terminfo* facility performs the same basic functions as the *termcap* database. The main difference is that after a *terminfo* entry has been written, it is compiled. The text file *terminfo.src* contains the entries in source format similar to */etc/termcap*.

/usr/lib/terminfo is a directory that contains subdirectories for the numbers 1-9 and each letter of the alphabet. In these subdirectories are distributed the object files for terminals beginning with that letter or number.

Some of the files in */usr/lib/terminfo/a* are:

```
adm3a
adm3a+
adm42
adm5
```

Each of these files is a *terminfo* entry for a terminal. Some of the files are linked so that the same "root" entry is available under different names.

Like *termcap*, it is possible to access individual capabilities described in a *terminfo* entry, although access might be more difficult since you are working with object code. If the special functions that access terminal-dependent variables are available on your system, they should be described under "TERM-INFO LEVEL ROUTINES" in your *curses(3)* documentation.

For More Information

This handbook cannot cover all that you need to know about *termcap* and *terminfo*, both of which are more complicated than *curses*.

If you are unfamiliar with either of these facilities, here is what you need to do:

1. Find out which database facility your system currently uses.

2. Examine the *<curses.h>* file and the *curses(3)* documentation in the UNIX manual to determine whether *curses* is implemented to use *termcap* or *terminfo*.

3. Become familiar with the kinds of terminal capabilities that are described in the database. See the documentation for *terminfo(4)* or *termcap(5)* in the UNIX manual shipped with your system.

4. Make sure that the entries for the terminals on your system are complete and work properly.

If your program responds awkwardly or not at all on certain terminals, test the entry for that terminal. Each terminal must have a correct *termcap* or *terminfo* entry for *curses* to work.

If your system maintains current entries for terminals in the *termcap* database, instead of *terminfo*, but *curses* is implemented so that it depends upon *terminfo*, you may have some problems getting programs to run on certain terminals.

The quickest solution to this mismatch is to check the *terminfo* database for the terminals that are used on your system. If these entries exist, they may work properly and the problem is solved, at least while running the program on the current set of terminals.

Even if you can't find the exact terminal entry, experiment with entries for different but similar terminals. Also, the terminal itself may be capable of emulating one of the more common entries, such as "tvi920" or "vt100".

In cases where suitable entries are found for some, but not all, of the terminals on the system, you may want to test for the terminal type inside your program. You can assign a default terminal type or determine a *terminfo* terminal type that you know to be compatible with the user's terminal.

Another avenue to explore is to see if the old curses library that uses *termcap* is still supported. For instance, one system that used *terminfo* as the standard database had changed the old curses header file to *<ocurse.h>* and the old curses library was named *libocurse.a*

There are also available (from various sources including the AT&T UNIX Toolchest) *termcap to terminfo* conversion programs. Such programs should not take too long to write on your own, although having to learn both *termcap* and *terminfo* may take some time.

To learn about the *termcap* capabilities, read the Nutshell Handbook *"Reading and Writing Termcap Entries."* A future Nutshell title on *terminfo* is planned for the series.

Examining the Header File

curses is made up of a library of procedures in */usr/lib* and a header file */usr/include/curses.h*. The library contains the compiled procedures while the header file contains definitions of the data types you will need.

The header file must be included in your program so that you can refer to the *curses* data types.

At the start of your file, add the line:

```
#include   <curses.h>
```

Global Variables and Defines

A library package not only contains functions; it also contains global variables in the source file and pre-processor #define instructions in the header file.

Let's look at what's contained in the header file. Compare the exact contents of */usr/include/curses.h* on your own system with the examples described below.

<curses.h> includes other header files which are read into your file as well:

```
# include   <stdio.h>

# include   <sgtty.h>
```

Your program will compile more efficiently if you do not include *<stdio.h>* and *<sgtty.h>* a second time. It is a good idea to check which other header files are already included in <curses.h>.

The WINDOW data structure is defined in *<curses.h>*. The external variables *curscr* and *stdscr* are also declared. The WINDOW structure that is used to define *stdscr* and *curscr* was described in Chapter 1.

<curses.h> contains the declarations for a number of constants and types which are generally available for use in your program. The values of these variables might be different on your system.

```
# define   bool  char
# define   reg   register

# define   ERR   (0)  /* returned if function fails */
# define   OK    (1)  /* returned if function succeeds */
# define   TRUE  (1)  /* Boolean true */
# define   FALSE (0)  /* Boolean false */
```

LINES and COLS are two variables that are available to specify the length and width of the screen. If you do not set them in your program, the length and width of the terminal are taken from the terminal database.

The header file also handles declaring variables for the terminal capabilities read in from the *termcap* or *terminfo* database. There may also be special constants defined for certain terminal features such as for a keypad, video attributes or graphics capabilities specifically available on a system.

Three terminal-related variables are declared in *<curses.h>*. They can be used in procedures that test and/or reset the terminal type:

Def_term	Used to set a default terminal type. For instance, the default terminal type could be assigned when **initscr()** is unable to find the TERM variable in the user's environment.
My_term	Used to override any terminal type setting and use instead the default terminal type defined in "Def_term". "My_term" could be a vanilla entry assigned to terminals not found in the database.
ttytype	Used to store the name of the current terminal type.

Pseudo-functions

Pseudo-functions (or macros) are functions that don't really exist. They are lookalike functions when they are in the uncompiled code, but in the *curses.h* header file, they are the argument of a #define, and are replaced by the pre-processor before they reach the compiler proper.

curses makes extensive use of pseudo-functions. This means that there are actually fewer functions to learn because you only have to learn the root functions. The pseudo-functions use a consistent naming and argument pattern, making them even easier to use. A disadvantage is that pseudo-functions will never show up in the compiled assembly code, a trace or symbolic debugger. You will find pseudo-functions in the *<curses.h>* header file, not in the *curses* source code.

If there can be many windows at once, and if windows are independent, then procedures must take as an argument a pointer to the window that they are to act upon. However, since one often works with only the default window, there is a set of pseudo-functions that affect *stdscr* automatically.

For instance:

> **refresh()** refreshes *stdscr*

addch() adds a character to *stdscr*

move() moves the cursor in *stdscr*

For each of these pseudo-functions, there is a function that takes a pointer to a window as an argument, and so can be used to make changes to any window. These functions are prefixed with a 'w' for window specific. For example:

wrefresh()

waddch()

wmove()

The window pointer is always the first argument. In fact, the automatic *stdscr* pseudo-functions are simply #defines that call the real "window-specific" function with *stdscr* as the window argument. The preprocessor writes in the true value of the function. If you look in *<curses.h>*, you will see the lines which do this #define.

```
#define addch(CH)    waddch(stdscr, CH)
```

A second group of pseudo-functions use #defines to reduce lengthy code. These pseudo-functions are prefixed with "mv". They move the logical cursor *and* do an I/O operation. For example:

```
#define mvaddch(Y,X,CH)        mvwaddch(stdscr, Y, X, CH)
#define mvwaddch(WIN,Y,X,CH)   wmove(WIN, Y, X); \
                               waddch(WIN, CH)
```

Note that the prefix "mv" comes before the prefix "w", but the WIN argument comes before the Y, X move coordinates. Also, note that the Y coordinate is given before the X coordinate. This is true for all *curses* functions.

Pseudo-functions are also used to define **getyx()**, **inch()**, **clearok()**, **leaveok()**, **scrollok()**, and **flushok()**.

3
The Curses Library

Introduction

This chapter describes groups of related functions in the *curses* library. A sample program is used to illustrate how a set of *curses* functions can work together to create a useful result with minimum work.

The sample program builds part of a screen driver for a spreadsheet program. It is designed so that each piece of code uses only the commands that have already been described. In places, this results in non-optimal code. The spreadsheet program is not complete. Adding defensive code to handle any user input would make it excessively long for inclusion here.

Check your UNIX documentation for the complete list of functions in the *curses* library. It is possible that some functions may be implemented differently or not at all on your system. Additional functions may be also available.

Using the Curses Library

To use *curses* library, you must include the header file in your program so that you can refer to the *curses* data types, and you must tell the linker (either through the compiler or the loader) where to find the *curses* functions.

Your source program must have the line:

```
#include    <curses.h>
```

and it must be compiled with

    cc [*flags*] **-lcurses** *file*

or load with

    ld [*flags*] **-lcurses** *file*

If *curses* is set up to use *termcap*, you should add the option **-ltermlib**. This will make the linker resolve references in the *curses* and *termlib* libraries, linking in the *curses* functions you use.

For instance, to compile the sample program used in this chapter the following command line is executed:

```
% cc spreadsheet.c -lcurses
```

A shell script to call the compiler with the library arguments is a good way to save typing while you debug.

The Spreadsheet Program

A sample program is used throughout this chapter to give examples of code containing many of the functions in the *curses* library. Please remember that this program was designed to illustrate *curses* rather than meet the requirements of a particular application.

This section describes the output that the spreadsheet program displays on the terminal screen. Later in this chapter, you will examine the individual sections of this program in relation to a particular group of *curses* functions. The complete program listing appears at the end of this handbook.

The first part of the program initializes *curses* for a particular terminal. It also sets up a procedure for exiting from the program and resetting the terminal so that it works normally outside of *curses*.

After initialization, the program begins to enter characters into the *stdscr*, a character array. Functions are called to design a box, move the logical cursor, and add strings that make up ID line. When *stdscr* is refreshed, the box is displayed on the screen with the ID line inside it.

Then the program prepares for user input by setting the terminal input modes. For instance, echo mode is set so that each character that the user types is displayed on the screen. A string, containing the input prompt, is then sent to the screen that asks the user to supply a filename.

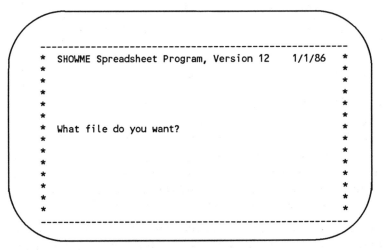

After the user supplies the filename, a prompt asks the user to enter a password.

```
Six-character password?
```

Prior to displaying this string, the input mode **noecho()** is called so that the user's password is not echoed on the screen. When the sixth character is typed, the password is verified.

The Curses Library   27

"OK" is displayed if the password is correct and the screen is cleared.

Then the spreadsheet workspace is created on the screen. Rows and columns are marked by letters and numbers. This workspace is actually a sub-window of *stdscr*. Changes can be made in the workspace independent of *stdscr*, and those changes will be displayed whenever *stdscr* is refreshed.

In this workspace, a group of new windows are created, corresponding to individual cells in the spreadsheet. As shown below, each cell is filled with a number.

	1	2	3	4	5	6	7	
	*							*
a	00	02	03	04	05	06	07	
	*							*
b	11	12	13	14	15	16	17	
	*							*
c	21	22	23	24	25	26	27	
	*							*
d	31	32	33	34	35	36	37	
	*							*
e	41	42	43	44	45	46	47	
	*							*
f	51	52	53	54	55	56	57	
	*							*
g	61	62	63	64	65	66	67	
	*							*

Lastly, a procedure is set up to refresh only those cells that are currently positioned in the workspace. Using a sub-window made up of a group of new windows divides the screen into separate areas that can be controlled individually.

At this point in the program, procedures need to be written to allow the user to do the work usually done with a spreadsheet. What this screen driver accomplishes, using the *curses* library, is to provide for optimized screen updating so that users can see their work on the terminal screen.

The Curses Functions

When you are introduced to *curses*, it is natural to learn about the simpler pseudo-functions like **refresh()** rather than the more general root functions like **wrefresh()**. You can understand how the root functions work once you learn the pseudo-functions. The pseudo-function automatically applies the window-specific root function on the standard screen (*stdscr*).

There is only one major difference in working with windows other than the standard screen: *stdscr* is always a full window while other windows can be much smaller.

Obviously, some of the concerns one has when applying functions to small windows are irrelevant when describing the pseudo-functions. Nonetheless, rather than go through each of the root functions separately, we will describe the problems presented by the root function on a small window along with the *stdscr* pseudo-functions.

The basic order in which functions are described in this section is:

1. beginning and ending work with *curses*,

2. accepting input and producing output,

3. working with multiple windows,

4. using miscellaneous and terminal-related functions.

Initialize and Terminate Curses

> **initscr()** Initialize *curses*
> **endwin()** End *curses*

Before you can use a window, you have to initialize it. When you create a window, your program must close the window before exiting to restore the terminal settings.

initscr()

initscr() creates two windows: *stdscr* and *curscr*. **initscr()** also calls **setterm()** to read in the terminal capability information from either the *termcap* or *terminfo* database.

The general practice is to call **initscr()** after checking for startup errors and when your program is sure that the user really wants to use windows.

Two of the error conditions that cause **initscr()** to return ERR are when:

1. There is not enough space available when **initscr()** allocates space for *stdscr*.

2. The function cannot find the environment variable TERM or it is unable to find the correct database entry for the terminal.

endwin()

endwin() should be called when your program is finished. This function undoes whatever manipulations *curses* has done to your terminal, returning your terminal modes to their original state.

The space taken up by *initscr* and *curscr* will be deallocated when the program terminates.

Example: Initialization

The first part of the sample program shows **initscr()** and **endwin()** in context.

```
#include <curses.h>
#include <signal.h>

main()
{
    int die();

/*      if (startup() != ERR)  startup unwritten */

/*              init stdscr, curscr and terminal */
```

30   *Programming with Curses*

(margin handwritten note: initscr() return NULL not ERR)

```
        initscr();
/*              call die() if get interrupt    */

        signal(SIGINT, die);

/*          spreadsheet function defined later  */

        spreadsheet();
        die();
}
die()
{
/*                  ignore interrupts    */

        signal(SIGINT, SIG_IGN);

/*              move cursor to lower left    */

        mvcur(0, COLS -1, LINES-1, 0);

/*              make terminal the way it was    */

        endwin();
        exit(0);                    /* exit normally */
}
```

startup() is an undefined user function that is commented out so that the sample program can run. **spreadsheet()** will be defined later on in this section.

signal() and **exit()** are standard C functions. **signal()** is a procedure for handling certain kinds of signals such as interrupts. **signal(SIGINT, die)** says to call **die()** when it receives a keyboard interrupt — this is a common way to end a program using windows because it works no matter where you are in the code.

die() executes **signal(SIGINT, SIGIGN)** to reset the system so that it ignores interrupts. **exit(0)** terminates a program without error. **mvcur()** is a *curses* function which moves the physical cursor. Here it moves the cursor to the lower left.

Cursor Location Utilities

move(y,x)	Move logical cursor to (y,x) in *stdscr*.
getyx(win,y,x)	Put location of logical cursor of *win* into *y* and *x*.
inch()	Get character at logical cursor in *stdscr*.
leaveok(win, flag)	Set _leave in *win* to *flag*.

This group of functions is used to determine the location of the logical cursor.

move(y,x)
  int y, x;

move() moves the location of the logical cursor in *stdscr*. Since all output is directed through this marker, move is an essential operation.

move() is often used in the form of the "mv" prefix macros that call the **move()** function followed by an output function. The (y,x) arguments given in **move()** are relative to the window, not the screen. The coordinates are based on the upper left corner of the window being (0,0). This is the same as (_cury, _curx) which stores the location of the logical cursor.

move() is really a #define macro for **wmove()** which takes a WINDOW* as its first argument. Do not confuse **move()** with **mvcur()** or **mvwin()**.

getyx(win,y,x)
*WINDOW *win;*
int y, x;

getyx() is another #define macro that returns the (*y,x*) location of the logical cursor of the specified window. The coordinates are interpreted in the same way as **move()**, based on the upper left corner of the window being (0,0). Because of the way the **getyx()** macro is written, *y* and *x* must be integer variables and not addresses of integer variables.

inch()

inch() returns the character that is at the location of the logical cursor in the screen image array. This is the only way to look at the screen image array. **inch()** is a #define macro for **winch(***stdscr***)**, where winch is the root function that gets the character at the logical cursor of the given window.

leaveok(win, flag)
*WINDOW *win;*
bool flag;

leaveok() sets the boolean value _**leave** to *flag* in the given window. As explained in "THE WINDOW STRUCTURE" section, _leave tells **refresh()** what to do with the physical and logical cursor after it has finished updating a screen.

If _leave is set, the logical cursor is moved to the final location of the physical cursor after the **refresh()**. This will be one past the location of the last character that **refresh()** had to change. If _leave is FALSE, the physical cursor will be left at the location of the logical cursor after the **refresh()**. Either way, the physical and logical cursors will end up at the same location.

Adding Characters to the Screen Image

addch(ch)	Add a character to *stdscr*.
addstr(str)	Add a string to *stdscr* by calling **addch()**.
printw(fmt, arg1, arg2, ...)	Formatted print to *stdscr* by calling **addstr()**.
insch(ch)	Insert a character into *stdscr*.
insertln()	Insert a line above current line in *stdscr*.
box(win, vert, hor)	Draw box at edge of *win*.
refresh()	Update screen to look like current *stdscr*.

addch(ch)
  char ch;

addch() adds a single character to *stdscr*. It is important to understand **addch()** because it does the work for **addstr()** and **printw()**.

It adds the character at the present location of the logical cursor and then moves that logical cursor one space to the right. The original contents of that location are overwritten by **addch()** (compare to **insch()**).

If this causes the logical cursor to go off the right end of the window, **addch()** checks the boolean flag _scroll in WINDOW to see if the window allows scrolling (see **scrollok()**). If scrolling is allowed, the logical cursor is moved to the right edge of the next line. If scrolling is prohibited, **addch()** returns ERR.

There are a few special characters **addch()** has to handle:

\t   If the character added is a tab, **addch()** adds up to eight space characters until the logical cursor has reached a horizontal location divisible by eight.

\r   If the character is a carriage return, **addch()** moves the logical cursor to the left end of the line. It does not echo a newline under any circumstances.

\b   If the character is a backspace, the logical cursor is moved backwards, one space to the left. No characters are added to the screen image.

\n   If the character is a newline, **addch()** clears the rest of the line, and moves the cursor to the same horizontal position on the next line. If this would move the logical cursor off the bottom of the window, and if the window is allowed to logical scroll (with the boolean _scroll flag set), the window will do a logical scroll up, losing the top line.

If the character causes the logical cursor to go off the right edge of the window, **addch()** automatically wraps it to the first character of the next line. If this would move the logical cursor out of the screen image, the window tries to perform a logical scroll.

addstr(str)
    *char *str*;

addstr() adds a string by multiple calls to **addch()**.

printw(fmt, arg1, arg2, ...)
    *char *fmt*;

printw() is a formatted print which interprets its arguments using the same syntax as the standard C function **printf()**. It also makes calls to **addch()** to actually add the characters to *stdscr*.

insch(ch)
    char ch;

insch() inserts the given character at the logical cursor. The main difference between **insch()** and **addch()** is that **insch()**

does not overwrite the character that was below the logical cursor; **addch()** does. Because **addstr()** and **printw()** call **addch()**, they also overwrite the old character.

With **insch()**, the original character at that location is shifted one space to the right, along with the rest of the line. The last character on the line is lost even if the window can scroll.

One other difference: **insch()** does not move the logical cursor, while **addch()** moves it one space to the right.

insertln()

insertln() is analogous to **insch()**. **insertln()** inserts a complete, blank line at the line which the logical cursor is on. The existing contents of the line, and every line after it, are shifted down one line. The bottom line of the window is lost. The logical cursor is left in its original position.

box(win, vert, hor)
   WINDOW *win;
   char vert, hor;

box() is a function which draws a box around the edge of the window. One of its arguments is *hor*, the horizontal character and the other is *ver*, the vertical character.

For example, box(*stdscr*, '-','*') will draw a box around the *stdscr* that consists of horizontal lines made with "-" and vertical lines made with "*". It looks like the one below, except it would be the full size of the screen.

```
- - - - - - - - - - - - - - - - - - - - - - - - - - - - - - - - - - - - - - - -
*                                                                             *
*                                                                             *
*                                                                             *
*                                                                             *
*                                                                             *
*                                                                             *
*                                                                             *
- - - - - - - - - - - - - - - - - - - - - - - - - - - - - - - - - - - - - - - -
```

box() works by adding the horizontal and vertical characters to their appropriate places in the screen image array.

There is nothing to stop the overwriting of these characters by a function called later. If you want to make sure the box will be preserved, make a box and then create a subwindow that sits inside the box, and work in the inner window.

Note that **box()** takes a window as an argument, while all the other functions in this group do not. **box()** is the only true function; all the others are pseudo-functions. The real functions are **waddch()**, **waddstr()**, **wprintw()**, and **wrefresh()** which all take a *WINDOW as their first argument in addition to their regular arguments. The preprocessor replaces the pseudo-functions with the real function that takes *stdscr* as its first argument.

refresh()

refresh() is the essential function. All the functions above change only the screen image, not what is being displayed. **refresh()** causes the screen to be changed so that it displays the current screen image.

The algorithm for **refresh()** was discussed in Chapter 1. The two key points are that it is window specific and that it tries to do as little redisplay as possible.

Example: Output

This part of the example demonstrates the output functions:

```
#define VERSION 12

spreadsheet()
{
    char filename[20];

    intro(VERSION);        /* print first screen */
/*                         initialize input modes */
    initinput();
/*                  read in file, check password */
```

```
        getfileandpw(filename);

/*              create the fields for spreadsheet */

        makefields();
/*                      makefields also calls driver */
}

/* intro() prints an initial screen */

intro(version)
int version;
{
    int x1, x2, y;
/*                      make box around the screen  */

    box(stdscr, '*', '-');
    move(1,2);
    addstr("SHOWME Spreadsheet Program, version: ");
    getyx(stdscr, y, x1);
    printw("%d", version);
    getyx(stdscr, y, x2);
    while (x2++ - x1 < 6)
        addch(' ');
    addstr("1/1/86");
/*                          send stdscr to terminal */
    refresh();
}
```

spreadsheet() is the driver for the sample program. It calls some functions which will be defined later. **intro()** prints an introductory screen, using several different output commands. It also uses the **getyx()** command so that it can print the version number in a fixed width field.

Standout Mode

> **standout()**   Begin standout mode.
> **standend()**   End standout mode.

One of the _flags in the WINDOW structure is _STAN-
DOUT. It tells **addch()** whether characters should be added
so that they "standout", or whether they should be in normal mode. You can turn standout on, add some characters,

turn standout off, add some more, etc. *curses* will keep track of which characters should be in standout mode and which should be normal.

Standout mode is whatever special highlighting the terminal can do, as defined in the terminal's database entry. If the terminal has no standout mode, it tries to underline instead, and if it can't underline, *curses* gives up and displays the character in normal mode.

standout()
and **standend()**

standout() and **standend()** are pseudo-functions, calling **wstandout()** and **wstandend()** with *stdscr* as the window argument.

Standout mode is off when you use **initscr()** to create *curscr* and *stdscr*, or when you use **newwin()** to create a new window. However, when you use **subwin()** to create a sub-window, the sub-window inherits the standout mode of its parent. Like all children, the sub-window is independent, and can change its inherited standout mode.

The mechanism *curses* uses is instructive. Terminals have standout modes that are turned on and off by control strings. Once standout mode has been turned on by one control string, characters are displayed in standout mode until the the terminal receives its "standout off" control string.

There is no alternate character set for standout characters. However, an alternate character set is exactly what *curses* needs. To allow standout to be turned on and off at random, *curses* must encode standout information with the character in the screen image.

curses uses the highest order bit of the byte to signify standout, leaving seven bits to encode the character itself. If that standout bit is set to one, the character will be displayed in standout mode; if it is zero, the character is normal.

The Curses Library   39

redisplay() makes the conversion between the alternate character set, required by *curses*, and the standout on/off control codes, required by the terminal. **redisplay()** looks at each character before it sends it to the screen, decides whether it is in standout mode or not, and sends the control string to affect standout appropriately.

Getting Characters from the Terminal

getch()	Get a character from the terminal.
getstr(str)	Get a string from the terminal.
scanw(fmt, arg1, arg2, ...)	Formatted input from the terminal like **scanf()**.

getch() and **getstr()** are simple functions. **getch()** gets a character from the terminal. In fact, it calls **getchar()**, the standard UNIX I/O function, to actually get the character. In addition, if the terminal is not in rawmode or crmode, it puts the terminal into crmode while it gets the character. The key to understanding terminal input is understanding the input modes. See the section on Input Modes for a description of rawmode and crmode.

getch()

getch() checks the boolean value _echoit to see if it should echo the character (see **echo()**, and **noecho()**). If _echoit is TRUE, **getch()** calls **addch()** to add the character at the logical cursor. Remember that **addch()** overwrites the old character and increments the cursor. Also, note that **addch()** handles some characters in a special way. For instance, a tab is stored in the screen image as a number of blanks. If the screen driver is echoing these characters, it may display these characters in a different form from what is stored in the screen image. The next **refresh()** will make the screen identical to the screen image.

Of course, **getch()** is a pseudo-function which is replaced by **wgetch(**_stdscr_**)**. It is easy to misinterpret what getting a character through a window means. When you use **wgetch()** to get a character through a window, the character will be echoed in that window (provided that window's _echoit flag is set). **wgetch()** is not affected by the location of the physical cursor on the screen. There is only one keyboard from which all characters must come, no matter where the physical cursor may be.

getstr(str)
  char *str;

getstr() calls **getch()** until it returns a newline or an EOF (end of file) character, or an error occurs. The string is read in to the array pointed to by *str, so be sure that this array is large enough to absorb all the characters that will be input. getstr(str) is a #define macro for **wgetstr(**_stdscr_, str**)**.

scanw(fmt, arg1, arg2, ...)
  char *fmt;

scanw() is to **scanf()** as **printw()** is to **printf()**. It uses the argument conventions of the standard I/O routine **scanf()**, just as **printw()** uses the conventions of **printf()**. **scanw()** calls **getch()** to get the actual characters, so **getch()** processes these characters as it always does. **scanw()** is a #define macro for wscanw(_stdscr_, ...) that will echo input (if _stdscr->_echoit is set) to the _stdscr_.

Input Modes

crmode()	Control input mode: ^S, ^Q, ^C, ^Y go to kernel. Also **cbreak()**.
nocrmode()	End control input mode. Also **nocbreak()**.
raw()	Raw input mode: no processing by the kernel.

noraw()	End raw input mode.
echo()	Echo input mode: characters echo on screen and in window.
noecho()	End echo input mode.
nl()	Set terminal to do <RETURN> after <LINEFEED>.
nonl()	Don't do <RETURN> after <LINEFEED>.

The various input modes are distinguished by how much character processing is done automatically by the kernel. You can choose between default mode, where the system kernel buffers input as usual, or crmode or raw mode, where *curses* controls input. Echo mode or nl mode can be set simultaneously with default, crmode, or raw mode. Your code should first change to crmode or raw mode (or rarely, stay in default mode). It should then specify **echo()** or **noecho()** and **nl()** or **nonl()** as you desire. You can change modes later for special purposes.

curses begins in default mode, and will return to default mode if you turn off any modes you have set. Default mode allows you to use character and line editing commands (which are handled by the kernel). To allow editing commands, the kernel buffers each line of input from the terminal. The major disadvantage is that to get a single character, you must wait until the line it is on has been completed. Default mode is seldom what you want.

crmode()
and **nocrmode()**

crmode() turns on control character (or cbreak) mode. In crmode, the terminal control characters are interpreted by the kernel, with all others sent directly to *curses*. The control characters that are interpreted include:

^S   Stop the screen display.

^Q   Continue the screen display.

^C   Interrupt signal.

^Y   Quit signal.

The most important difference between crmode and default mode is that the characters are not buffered in crmode, and so a single character is available to *curses* as soon as it is typed. This removes the major drawback of default mode, while still allowing you to send signals to your program. **nocrmode()** turns off **crmode()**.

raw()
and **noraw()**

raw() sets raw mode. In raw mode, the kernel does no processing or buffering of input, but passes it straight to *curses*. Raw mode is good if you do not want to handle interrupts and quits and would rather just ignore them. **noraw()** turns off raw mode.

echo()
and **noecho()**

echo() sets echo mode. Echo mode can be set with default mode, crmode, or raw mode. **echo()** sets both logical and physical echo. Logical echo means input characters are added to the window specified in the *curses* function that is getting the characters (see above). The characters are added to the window using **waddch()** and so are added at the logical cursor. Physical echo means characters are also echoed to the screen locally by your terminal. **noecho()** turns off physical and logical echo.

nl()
and **nonl()**

nl(), which sets newline mode, makes the terminal map a carriage return to a newline on input and output. Note that this mapping is done at the level of the terminal, not *curses*. Like echo mode, nl mode can be set with default, crmode or raw mode. (However, raw and cbreak mode do turn off newline mapping on character input.)

Newline mapping is convenient outside *curses*, and most terminals are operated in newline mapping mode. However, *curses* is more efficient if newline mapping is turned off, because *curses* can then use the linefeed character to move the cursor down without the side effect of moving to the start of the line. You should turn newline mapping off unless you have a special reason to have it on. **nonl()** turns off input and output newline mapping.

Example: Input

This part of the sample program demonstrates the input functions:

```
initinput()                   /* set up initial modes */
{
    raw();
    echo();
    nonl();
}

getfileandpw(filename)
char *filename;
{
    char passwd[6];
    int i = 0;
    mvaddstr(4,2, "What file do you want? ");
    refresh();
    while ((filename[i] = getch()) != '\r')
        i++;
    filename[i] = '\0';
    mvaddstr(3,2, "Six character Password? ");
    noecho();
    refresh();
    i = 0;
    while (i < 6)
        passwd[i++] = getch();
/*                                check password */
    if (passwdok(passwd)) {
        mvaddstr(4, 26, "OK");
    /*  readinfile(filename);  readinfile unwritten */
        refresh();
```

```
        }
    else {
        mvaddstr(4, 26, "NO");
        refresh();
        die();
        }
}
/*          Dummy function so that example will run */
passwdok(passwd)
char *passwd;
{
        return(1);
}
```

initinput() sets up the input modes. **getfileandpw()** reads the filename and a password from the user's input. Note that when it gets the filename, it replaces the carriage return with a null character, making the filename a string. Echoing is turned off while the password is typed in. **passwdok()** is a dummy function included so that this example code can be compiled.

Erasing and Clearing

delch()	Delete a single character and shift rest of line to left.
deleteln()	Delete a line, shifting lines up from below.
clrtoeol()	Erase line from logical cursor to edge of window.
clrtobot()	Erase from logical cursor to bottom of window.
erase()	Erase the window but don't clear screen.
clear()	Reset window to blanks and clear screen if necessary.
clearok(scr, flag)	Clear screen at next refresh but don't reset window.

First, note that except for **clearok()**, these are all pseudo-functions that call the root function (prefixed by a 'w') and apply them to *stdscr*.

Second, observe that these functions can be divided into two families. The first four functions make up one family. These functions affect the character under the logical cursor and, possibly, the characters to its left or on lower lines. These functions simply add blanks in various places.

The second family, made up of the last three functions, clears the entire screen. As well as adding blanks, they may also generate a clear screen sequence on the next refresh.

The first family is easy to understand, while the second can be confusing.

Third, realize how *curses* represents a blank screen. *curses* cannot use some of the shortcuts the physical terminal screen can. Every location in the screen image character array must have a value. *curses* uses a space character, not a null character, when it wants to make a space blank.

To erase a line, *curses* fills the line with spaces. To erase an entire window, *curses* fills the whole screen image with spaces. Since another name for the space character is a "blank", this is called "blanking a line" or "blanking a screen."

delch()

delch() is simple. It deletes the character under the logical cursor, shifts the tail of the line that follows left one space, and puts a blank in at the end of the line. If you delete characters from a line that has run over and scrolled onto the next line of the window, the routine does not know enough to do a backward scroll. It will not move the left edge of the lower line back onto the right edge of the upper line.

deleteln()

deleteln() parallels **delch()**: it deletes a whole line and shifts all lower lines up. It will do this shift even on windows that cannot scroll. The last line of the window will be set to blanks.

clrtoeol()

clrtoeol() blanks out all the characters on the line from the logical cursor to the right edge of the window. The logical cursor is not moved.

clrtobot()

clrtobot() calls clrtoeol(), blanking from the logical cursor to the edge of the window. It then blanks every character on every line of the window below the logical cursor. The logical cursor is not moved.

erase(), clearok(), and clear() are easy to confuse. There are three functions to clear the screen because there are actually two ways to clear the screen. The first way is to fill the screen image array with blanks, and then refresh the screen. This is relatively slow, because refresh() must redisplay the screen character by character, finding every non-blank character on the screen, and replacing it with a blank.

The second way is to send the terminal its clear control code, which automatically clears the screen. This "hardware" clear is fast because it is built into the terminal. A hardware clear is also sure, because no matter how the screen has been filled with characters from I/O or modem noise, it will be erased. *curses* uses the boolean _clear to indicate that refresh() should generate a hardware clear screen for that window the next time it is called (see the section "The Window Structure"). The three screen-clearing commands provide combinations of these two methods.

erase()

erase() fills the screen image with blanks, and does not set the _clear flag. This is not very useful for windows like *stdscr* and *curscr* that fill the entire screen. The window-oriented werase() is good for windows that only occupy part of the screen. (The hardware clear will always clear the entire screen.)

clearok(scr, flag)
  *WINDOW *scr;*
  bool flag;

clearok() is a simple pseudo-function that sets the _clear flag to the boolean value given. It is usually used to force a hardware clear but could also be used to set the hardware flag to FALSE to abort a hardware clear.

clearok() does not fill the screen image with blanks. Furthermore, **clearok()** does not check that the window fills the entire screen; it just sets the _clear flag. That check is done by **refresh()**, which will only clear the screen if the window occupies the full screen. (It does this by checking the _FULLWIN flag in _flags.)

After **refresh()** clears the screen, it then redisplays the non-blank contents of the window. **refresh()** also sets the _clear flag to FALSE. **clearok()** assures that the window is exactly the same as the current contents. If you are using multiple, small windows, setting the clear flag with **clearok()** will not help, because they are not full screens. In this case, you want to use clearok(*curscr*, TRUE) before you refresh a small window that will generate a hardware clear on the next refresh of any window, and then redraw the screen with the old *curscr* plus the new window that you refreshed.

clear()

clear() fills the screen with blanks and sets the _clear flag. In fact, the source code for clear is simply two function calls: one to **erase()**, the other to **clearok()**.

clear() is often used instead of **erase()** because it is easier: you don't have to think about whether the window is a complete screen or not because **refresh()** will decide for you. Good programming practice is to say what you mean. If you *know* that a window is not a full screen, use **erase()** instead of **clear()**. If you don't know, don't go to the trouble of checking the _FULLSCR flag to find out; simply use **clear()**. What this means is that when you are addressing a window by name and know that it is not a full screen, use **erase()**. Otherwise, someone may assume that since you used **clear()**, the window must be a full screen. As a final bonus, calling **erase()** in the first place is faster than an aborted hardware clear.

Creating and Removing Multiple Windows

newwin(lines,cols,y1,x1)	Create a new window.
subwin(win,lines,cols,y1,x1)	Create a sub-window.
delwin(win)	Delete *win* from existence.

Chapter 1 discussed multiple windows, and the difference between new windows and sub-windows. To repeat the major difference, new windows are independent windows in every way, while sub-windows share the screen image array of their parent window. This difference has consequences in the way the windows are affected by functions.

WINDOW *
newwin(lines,cols,y1,x1)
 int lines, cols, y1, x1;

newwin() creates a new window. The new window will have *lines* lines and *cols* columns, with the upper left corner located at (*y1, x1*). If you give the argument *lines*=0, the new window will go from *y1* to the bottom of the screen. Similarly, if *cols*=0, the new window will stretch from *x1* to the right margin of the screen. Windows may be as tall and thin, short and wide, or as small as single character.

newwin() returns the *WINDOW to the new window structure. The screen image in the new window is filled with blanks. The _flags are set automatically by the size and location of the new window.

Creating a new window requires a fair amount of memory (especially for the screen image array) and it is possible that the call to the system function **alloc()** to get this memory will fail. If so, or if the any part of the new window will not fit on the screen, **newwin()** will return NULL. Your program should check for NULL because you cannot blissfully ignore failure to allocate a window.

WINDOW *
subwin(win,lines,cols,y1,x1)
  WINDOW *win;*
  int lines,cols,y1,x1;

subwin() creates a sub-window. *win* is a pointer to the parent window.

The other arguments are the same as in **newwin()**, except that *lines* and *cols* are interpreted relative to the parent window and not the terminal screen. That is, if *lines* or *cols* are zero, the sub-window is made to the bottom and/or right of the parent window. *y1* and *x1* are still interpreted relative to the screen as a whole.

The sub-window inherits the _STANDOUT, _FLUSH, _INSL, and _DELL flags of its parent, the _SUBWIN flag is set, and the _SCROLLWIN, _FULLWIN, _FULLLINE and _ENDLINE flags are determined by the size and position of the sub-window.

Note that there is no pointer in the sub-window to the parent window. The only connection the sub-window has to the parent is the shared screen image. Therefore, it is impossible for the sub-window to do any operations that would require knowing about its parent.

A sub-window is a real WINDOW, and may have sub-windows just as easily as the original parent window. Therefore, sub-windows may have sub-windows may have sub-windows, to any depth you desire. Each sub-window is created within the boundaries of its respective parent, and the whole family will use the original window's screen image.

Just as with **newwin()**, there must be enough memory available to allocate the structure, and the sub-window must fit entirely inside the parent window. If there is an error, **subwin()** returns NULL. As with **newwin()**, be sure to check for NULL.

delwin(win)
   WINDOW *win;

delwin() is a simple function: it deletes the specified window.

delwin() calls the system utility **free()** to return the space occupied by that window to the pool of available memory. If the window is a sub-window, **delwin()** does not **free()** the space occupied by its screen image; that screen image is still being used by the parent window. If the opposite is true, that the window is a parent, the screen image is released by **free()** and so all of its sub-windows are useless.

However, since parent windows do not know who or how many sub-windows there are, sub-windows are not automatically deleted. They will continue to occupy space, and their screen image will be undefined.

Because this can be a dangerous situation, you should be sure to call **delwin()** to delete all the sub-windows of a parent window. You should call **delwin()** to keep the number of active windows under control and to increase the amount of memory available to your program. For these reasons, **delwin()** is a good housekeeping function.

Window-Specific Functions

As you know, most functions that apply to *stdscr* are really #define macros for a generalized window function. The transition from the *stdscr* functions to the window-specific functions is an easy one to make.

Syntactically, the root functions have the character 'w' added to their name and take a *WINDOW as their first argument. (Some functions, such as **box()** do not have a pseudo-function and so do not need the prefix 'w'. They still take a *WINDOW as their first argument.)

Remember that the functions are limited to the window. For example, if you have a 5x5 sub-window pointed to by "smallw" in the middle of the screen, and you make the following call:

```
waddstr(smallw, "abcdefgh")
```

you will get something that looks like this:

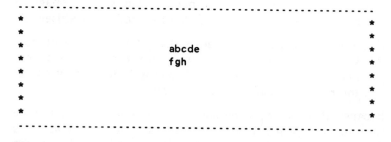

The line-wrap will be done entirely within the window. This logical scroll, as well as insert lines, delete lines and erase work within that window alone. To windows, the world ends at the border of their character array, whether they fill the full screen like *stdscr* or are only a single character.

For the sake of space, the 'w' prefixed functions will not be described in full. They are included in the Quick Reference at the end of this Handbook.

Manipulating Multiple Windows

overlay(win1,win2)	Overlay *win1* on *win2*, excluding blanks.
overwrite(win1,win2)	Overwrite *win1* on *win2*, including blanks.
touchwin(win)	Make next refresh rewrite whole window.
mvwin(win, y, x)	Move top left corner of *win* to (*y*,*x*).

overlay(win1,win2)
  WINDOW *win1, *win2;

overwrite(win1,win2)
  WINDOW *win1, *win2;

overlay() and **overwrite()** are a pair of functions with one minor difference. Both take two WINDOW pointers as arguments. Both copy the contents of the screen image of the first window into the screen image of the second window.

The top left corners of the two screen images are aligned, and the regions that overlap are copied. Areas that do not correspond are left alone. Neither window is moved, and no modes are changed. These functions only make changes to the screen image of the second window (and _firstch and _lastch which are adjusted in the second window to reflect those changes.) The first window is unaffected.

overlay() and **overwrite()** differ in how they handle spaces in the first window. **overlay()** does not copy blanks from the first window to the second. The result is that all the printing characters of the first window are "overlaid" on top of the second window, but the printing characters in the second window that are not covered are still visible.

overwrite() does copy blanks. The first window is copied in its entirety - blanks and all - into the second screen image. If the second screen image is larger in one or both dimensions than the first, the fringes of the second window will not be changed or erased.

touchwin(win)
  *WINDOW *win*;

touchwin() is a companion to **refresh()**. It sets _firstch = 0 and _lastch = (_maxx-1) for every line of the window. This tells **refresh()** that every location in the screen image might have been changed. **refresh()** will then check every character of the screen image against *curscr*, and display the character in the screen image whenever there is a mismatch.

When you are working with overlapping windows, you might want to display the contents of the window underneath. Since you haven't changed that window, **refresh()** would normally think that the screen is showing it "as is", not knowing that another window has been displayed over it. **touchwin()** forces it to redisplay the window in its entirety.

touchwin() is also useful when you have a window that contains several sub-windows. Without **touchwin()**, if you make changes in those sub-windows and wanted to refresh them all, you would have to **refresh()** them one by one. Instead, you can call **touchwin()** for the parent window; then **refresh()** the parent window. Since sub-windows share the character array of the parent window, all the changes made in the sub-windows will now be displayed when you **refresh()** the parent window. (If you had not called **touchwin()** on the parent window, **refresh()** would not have known to redisplay the changes because they were made through the sub-windows.)

Since **refresh()** compares the window to *curscr*, **touchwin()** will not force **refresh()** to overwrite stray characters that were output by echoed input or by **printf()** and other non-*curses* output. The best way to **refresh()** in this situation is to avoid the problem by calling **refresh()** after echoing input and to never use non-*curses* output functions.

The other alternative is to force a hardware clear screen with **clear()** or **clearok()**.

mvwin(win, y, x)
WINDOW *win;
int y, x;

mvwin() moves the whole window to a new location in the screen.

One of the fields in a WINDOW structure is a coordinate pair, (_begx, _begy), that indicates where the left corner of the window should be placed. mvwin() simply changes these values.

For a new window, this has the expected result: it causes the entire window to be displayed in the new location.

For a sub-window, however, this is very dangerous. The sub-window points into the array of the parent window. To move it fully, all those pointers would have to be adjusted, and the old contents of the sub-window copied to the new location. Because the sub-window does not know the size or location of its parent window, it cannot adjust those pointers. Consequently, the sub-window will be displayed in the new location, but will still be using the memory in its original position. Usually, this is a disaster.

Don't confuse mvwin() with wmove(), which moves the logical cursor inside a window, or movcur(), which moves the real cursor on the screen.

Example: Multiple Windows

This part of the example demonstrates multiple windows. A sub-window is created in the *stdscr* to serve as a workspace. This workspace can be erased and scrolled independently of *stdscr*, but will be refreshed if *stdscr* is refreshed.

A ten-by-ten array of new windows are created for the actual fields that the spreadsheet program would work in. They are initialized with their column and row numbers; in a real program, the file would be read in.

The function **reffields()** prints only the fields that are visible on the screen. The external variables _top and _left hold the indices of the top left field.

```
int _top; _left;

makefields()
{
    WINDOW *worksp, *field[10][10];
    int i, j;
    extern int _left, _top;

    worksp = subwin(stdscr, LINES -2, COLS -2, 1, 1);

/*              create a sub-window to work in  */

    werase(worksp);
    wmove(worksp, 1, 0);
    waddstr(worksp, "\t0\t1\t2\t3\t4\t5\t6\t7");
    wmove(worksp, 3, 0);
    waddch(worksp, 'a');
    mvwaddch(worksp, 5, 0, 'b');
    mvwaddch(worksp, 7, 0, 'c');
    mvwaddch(worksp, 9, 0, 'd');
    mvwaddch(worksp,11, 0, 'e');
    mvwaddch(worksp,13, 0, 'f');
    mvwaddch(worksp,15, 0, 'g');
    mvwaddch(worksp,17, 0, 'h');
    mvwaddch(worksp,19, 0, 'i');
    mvwaddch(worksp,21, 0, 'j');
    wrefresh(worksp);

/*                      display border of workspace */
    for (i = 0; i < 10; i++)
        for (j = 0; j < 10; j++) {
            field[i][j] = newwin(1, 7, 4+2*i, 7+8*j);
            wprintw(field[i][j], "%d %d", i, j);
/*                      create fields to work in  */
        }
    _left = 0; _top = 0;
    reffields(field);
/*  iodriver(worksp, field);   iodriver unwritten */
}
/*      reffields refreshes the fields currently
                        positioned in the workspace  */
reffields(field)
WINDOW *field[10][10];
{
```

```
        int i, j;
        extern int _top, _left;
        for (i = _top; i <= _top + 7; i++)
            for (j = _left; j <= _left + 7; j++) {
                touchwin(field[i][j]);
                wrefresh(field[i][j]);
            }
}
```

Miscellaneous Functions

mvcur(oldy,oldx,newy,newx)	Move the physical cursor from old (y,x) to new (y,x).
unctrl(ch)	Return printable string when given a control character.
scrollok(win, flag)	Permit or prohibit logical scrolls in *win*.
scroll(win)	Scroll *win* up one line.

mvcur(oldy,oldx,newy,newx)
  int oldy,oldx,newy,newx;

mvcur() moves the physical cursor on the screen, as efficiently as possible. Its arguments are based on the upper left corner of the screen being (0,0).

If you do not know where the cursor is, you can still use **mvcur()** by saying that the cursor is at coordinates far from where it should go. If you do this, **mvcur()** will use an absolute cursor move command rather than a few relative steps.

It is dangerous to use **mvcur()** while you are working with windows, as it will separate the physical cursor from the logical cursor, with all the pitfalls described under "Some Potential Problems" in Chapter 1. Instead, you should use **move()** to move the logical cursor inside a window; then **refresh()** that window (with the _leave field FALSE). This will put the physical and the logical cursor at the desired location.

unctrl(ch)
  char ch;

unctrl() returns the two-character string "^*x*", (a carat ('^') followed by a printable character) when given the character CONTROL-*x*.

unctrl() is useful because most terminals interpret control characters in special ways: the familiar CONTROL-H is a backspace, CONTROL-I is often a tab, and other control characters may turn on special, terminal-dependent features.

Normally, you do not want to send a control character to the terminal. To *curses*, it is just another character in the screen image; to the terminal, it is some special command.

To use **unctrl()**, you must #include the *<unctrl.h>* header file in your program.

scrollok(win, flag)
  *WINDOW *win;*
    bool flag;

scrollok() sets the _scroll flag (see the section "The WINDOW Structure") in the specified window to TRUE or FALSE.

A window will try to do a logical scroll if an input string runs off the right edge of the last line of the window. A logical scroll deletes the top line of the window, moves all the lower lines up one line, inserts a new, blank line at the bottom of the window, and continues the string on that blank line.

The _scroll flag indicates whether logical scrolling is permitted. Logical scrolling does not require that the window include the whole bottom line so that the terminal can do a physical scroll (this is the function of the SCROLLOK flag).

Logical scrolling is done entirely by character manipulation in the screen image of the window. Therefore, any window, no matter how large or small, or where it is located, can be set to allow logical scrolling.

scroll(win)
   WINDOW *win;

scroll() actually does a logical scroll on the specified window (see scrollok() immediately above). scroll() is called automatically when a window needs to scroll. You will only need to call scroll() when it is the special effect you desire. scroll() scrolls the window up one line.

Low-level Termcap Routines

setterm(name)	Set the terminal capabilities from */etc/termcap*.
longname(termbuf,name)	Put the long name for your terminal into *name*.

curses is terminal independent, and thus must read and use the terminal capabilities stored in either *termcap* or *terminfo*. The capabilities are read in and used automatically so these functions are usually irrelevant. However, the low-level functions are available, so for completeness they are described here.

You must know the UNIX terminal-database facility to make sense of these capabilities.

setterm(name)
   char *name;

setterm() is called automatically by initscr(). initscr() gets the name of the terminal you are working on by looking at the environment variable $TERM.

setterm() is called with $TERM as the argument *name*. For instance, if *termcap* is used, setterm() looks up *name* in */etc/termcap* and reads the termcap entry into a character buffer called _tcbuf. **setterm()** then extracts the capabilities from _tcbuf to the external capability variables AM, BS, etc. You will not normally have to call **setterm()**.

longname(termbuf,name)
  char *termbuf, *name;

longname() is passed two character pointers: *termbuf* is a pointer to a character array that contains the entry for the terminal, and *name* is a pointer to an empty buffer. **longname()** extracts the terminal name from *termbuf*, copies it into *name*, and then returns a pointer to the first character in name.

longname() is called automatically by **initscr()**, and reads the terminal name from _tcbuf into the external variable *ttytype[ ]*. You will probably never use **longname()**.

Terminal Manipulation

gettmode()	Get tty status.
savetty()	Save tty status.
resetty()	Reset tty status stored by **savetty()**.

curses must do more than find out the capabilities and command sequences from the terminal database facility. It must also control the low-level terminal modes such as echoing, or mapping a new line on carriage returns.

This requires two sets of functions: the input mode functions described before and the tty functions described here. You will use the input mode functions. The tty functions are primarily used by the system itself. Like the terminal-level functions before, you will probably never need them. Consequently, they will be described briefly.

gettmode()

gettmode() is used to establish the current tty modes while in *curses*. It reads in the baud rate of the terminal into the variables _tty.sg_ospeed and _tty.sg_ispeed. It turns off the mapping of carriage returns to line feeds on output, and the expansion of tabs into spaces by the system.

savetty()
and **resetty()**

savetty() saves the tty status at the beginning of a session and resetty() restores it.

savetty() is called when *curses* begins to save the current tty settings. resetty() is called when *curses* ends to return the terminal modes to their settings as stored by savetty().

Sample Program

Below is the complete listing of the sample program that builds a screen driver for a spreadsheet program.

```
#include <curses.h>
#include <signal.h>

main()
{
    int die();

/*      if (startup() != ERR)  startup unwritten */

/*               init stdscr, curscr and terminal */

        initscr();

/*                  call die() if get interrupt   */

        signal(SIGINT, die);

/*               spreadsheet function defined later */

        spreadsheet();
        die();
}

die()
{
/*                        ignore interrupts   */

    signal(SIGINT, SIG_IGN);

/*                   move cursor to lower left */

    mvcur(0, COLS -1, LINES-1, 0);
```

```
/*               make terminal the way it was    */

    endwin();
    exit(0);                      /* exit normally   */
}

#define VERSION 12

spreadsheet()
{
    char filename[20];

    intro(VERSION);          /* print first screen */
/*                          initialize input modes */
    initinput();
/*                   read in file, check password */

    getfileandpw(filename);

/*             create the fields for spreadsheet */

    makefields();
/*                    makefields also calls driver */
}

/* intro() prints an initial screen */

intro(version)
int version;
{
    int x1, x2, y;
/*                    make box around the screen   */

    box(stdscr, '*', '-');
    move(1,2);
    addstr("SHOWME Spreadsheet Program, version: ");
    getyx(stdscr, y, x1);
    printw("%d", version);
    getyx(stdscr, y, x2);
    while (x2++ - x1 < 6)
        addch(' ');
    addstr("1/1/86");
/*                       send stdscr to terminal */
    refresh();
}
initinput()               /* set up initial modes */
{
    raw();
```

```
        echo();
        nonl();
}

getfileandpw(filename)
char *filename;
{
        char passwd[6];
        int i = 0;
        mvaddstr(4,2, "What file do you want? ");
        refresh();
        while ((filename[i] = getch()) != '\r')
            i++;
        filename[i] = '\0';
        mvaddstr(3,2, "Six character Password? ");
        noecho();
        refresh();
        i = 0;
        while (i < 6)
            passwd[i++] = getch();
/*                                      check password */
        if (passwdok(passwd)) {
            mvaddstr(4, 26, "OK");
   /*     readinfile(filename);  readinfile unwritten */
            refresh();
            }
        else {
            mvaddstr(4, 26, "NO");
            refresh();
            die();
            }
}
/*          Dummy function so that example will run */
passwdok(passwd)
char *passwd;
{
        return(1);
}

int _top; _left;

makefields()
{
        WINDOW *worksp, *field[10][10];
        int i, j;
        extern int _left, _top;

        worksp = subwin(stdscr, LINES -2, COLS -2, 1, 1);
```

```
/*              create a sub-window to work in   */

    werase(worksp);
    wmove(worksp, 1, 0);
    waddstr(worksp, "\t0\t1\t2\t3\t4\t5\t6\t7");
    wmove(worksp, 3, 0);
    waddch(worksp, 'a');
    mvwaddch(worksp, 5, 0, 'b');
    mvwaddch(worksp, 7, 0, 'c');
    mvwaddch(worksp, 9, 0, 'd');
    mvwaddch(worksp,11, 0, 'e');
    mvwaddch(worksp,13, 0, 'f');
    mvwaddch(worksp,15, 0, 'g');
    mvwaddch(worksp,17, 0, 'h');
    mvwaddch(worksp,19, 0, 'i');
    mvwaddch(worksp,21, 0, 'j');
    wrefresh(worksp);

/*                  display border of workspace */

    for (i = 0; i < 10; i++)
        for (j = 0; j < 10; j++) {
            field[i][j] = newwin(1, 7, 4+2*i, 7+8*j);
            wprintw(field[i][j], "%d %d", i, j);

/*                  create fields to work in   */
        }
    _left = 0; _top = 0;
    reffields(field);
/*  iodriver(worksp, field);   iodriver unwritten */
}

/*      reffields refreshes the fields currently
                    positioned in the workspace   */

reffields(field)
WINDOW *field[10][10];
{
    int i, j;
    extern int _top, _left;
    for (i = _top; i <= _top + 7; i++)
        for (j = _left; j <= _left + 7; j++) {
            touchwin(field[i][j]);
            wrefresh(field[i][j]);
        }
}
```

Quick Reference

addch(ch)
char ch;
    Add a character to *stdscr*. [p. 34]

addstr(str)
char *str;
    Add a string to *stdscr* by calling **addch()**. [p. 35]

box(win, vert, hor)
WINDOW *win;
char vert, hor;
    Draw box at edge of *win*. [p. 36]

clear()
    Reset window to blanks and clear screen if necessary. [p. 48]

clearok(scr, flag)
WINDOW *scr; bool flag;
    Clear screen at next refresh but don't reset window. [p. 48]

clrtobot()
    Erase from logical cursor to bottom of window. [p. 47]

clrtoeol()
    Erase line from logical cursor to edge of window. [p. 47]

crmode()
    Control input mode: ^S, ^Q, ^C, ^Y go to kernel. Also **cbreak()**. [p. 42]

delch()
    Delete a single character and shift rest of line to left. [p. 46]

deleteln()
    Delete a line, shifting lines up from below. [p. 46]

delwin(win)
WINDOW *win;
    Delete *win* from existence. [p. 51]

echo()
> Echo input mode: characters echo on screen and in window. [p. 43]

endwin()
> End *curses*. [p. 30]

erase()
> Erase the window but don't clear screen. [p. 47]

getch()
> Get a character from the terminal. [p. 40]

getstr(str)
> *char *str;*
>> Get a string from the terminal. [p. 41]

gettmode()
> Get tty status. [p. 61]

getyx(win,y,x)
> *WINDOW *win;*
> *int y, x;*
>> Put location of logical cursor of *win* into *y* and *x*. [p. 33]

inch()
> Get character at logical cursor in *stdscr*. [p. 33]

initscr()
> Initialize *curses*. [p. 30]

insch(ch)
> *char ch;*
>> Insert a character into *stdscr*. [p. 35]

insertln()
> Insert a line above current line in *stdscr*. [p. 36]

leaveok(win, flag)
> *WINDOW *win; bool flag;*
>> Set _leave in *win* to *flag*. [p. 33]

longname(termbuf, name)
> *char *termbuf, *name;*
>> Put the long name for your terminal into *name*. [p. 60]

move(y,x)
> *int y, x;*
>> Move logical cursor to (y,x) in *stdscr*. [p. 32]

mvcur(oldy,oldx,newy,newx)
> *int oldy,oldx,newy,newx;*
>> Move the physical cursor from old (y,x) to new (y,x). [p. 57]

mvwin(win, y, x)
> *WINDOW *win;*
> *int y, x;*
>> Move top left corner of *win* to (y,x). [p. 55]

WINDOW *
newwin(lines,cols,y1,x1)
  int lines, cols, y1, x1;
    Create a new window
    of *lines x cols* starting
    at coordinates *y1,x1*.
    [p. 49]

nl()
    Set terminal to do
    <RETURN> after
    <LINEFEED>. [p. 43]

nocrmode()
    End control input
    mode. Also **noc-
    break()**. [p. 42]

noecho()
    End echo input mode.
    [p. 43]

nonl()
    Don't do <RETURN>
    after <LINEFEED>.
    [p. 43]

noraw()
    End raw input mode.
    [p. 43]

overlay(win1,win2)
  *WINDOW *win1, *win2;*
    Overlay *win1* on *win2*,
    excluding blanks.
    [p. 53]

overwrite(win1,win2)
  *WINDOW *win1, *win2;*
    Overwrite *win1* on
    win2, including
    blanks. [p. 53]

printw(fmt, arg1,arg2, ...)
  *char *fmt;*
    Formatted print to
    stdscr by calling
    addstr(). [p. 35]

raw()
    Raw input mode: no
    processing by the ker-
    nel. [p. 43]

refresh()
    Update screen to look
    like current *stdscr*.
    [p. 37]

resetty()
    Reset tty status stored
    by **savetty()**. [p. 61]

savetty()
    Save tty status. [p. 61]

scanw(fmt, arg1, arg2, ...)
  *char *fmt;*
    Formatted input from
    the terminal like
    scanf(). [p. 41]

scroll(win)
  *WINDOW *win;*
    Scroll *win* up one line.
    [p. 59]

scrollok(win, flag)
  *WINDOW *win;*
  bool flag;
    Permit or prohibit
    logical scrolls in *win*.
    [p. 58]

setterm(name)
char *name;
> Set the terminal capabilities from */etc/termcap*. [p. 59]

standend()
> End standout mode. [p. 39]

standout()
> Begin standout mode. [p. 39]

WINDOW *
subwin(win,lines,cols,y1,x1)
WINDOW *win;
int lines,cols,y1,x1;
> Create a sub-window in *win* of *lines x cols* starting at coordinates *y1,x1*. [p. 50]

touchwin(win)
WINDOW *win;
> Make next refresh rewrite whole window. [p. 54]

unctrl(ch)
char ch;
> Return printable string when given a control character. [p. 58]

Window-Specific Functions

These functions are some of the functions above applied to a window. A 'w' is placed before the function name, and the first argument is a pointer to the window.

waddch(win,ch)	winch(win)
waddstr(win,str)	winsch(win,c)
wclear(win)	winsertln(win)
wclrtobot(win)	wmove(win,y,x)
wclrtoeol(win)	wprintw(win,fmt,arg1,arg2, ...)
wdelch(win,c)	wrefresh(win)
wdeleteln(win)	wscanw(win,fmt,arg1,arg2, ...)
werase(win)	wstandend(win)
wgetch(win)	wstandout(win)
wgetstr(win,str)	

Move and Act Functions

These functions first move the cursor, then perform their action. The function names have a 'mv' placed before the corresponding function above.

mvaddch(y, x, ch)	mvwaddch(win, y, x, ch)
mvaddstr(y, x, str)	mvwaddstr(win, y, x, str)
mvdelch(y, x)	mvwdelch(win, y, x)
mvdeleteln(y, x)	mvwdeleteln(win, y, x)
mvinch(y, x)	mvwinch(win, y, x)
mvinsch(y, x, ch)	mvwinsch(win, y, x, ch)
mvinsertln(y, x)	mvwinsertln(win, y, x)

Colophon

Our look is the result of reader comments, our own experimentation, and distribution channels.

Distinctive covers complement our distinctive approach to UNIX documentation, breathing personality and life into potentially dry subjects. UNIX and its attendant programs can be unruly beasts. Nutshell Handbooks help you tame them.

The animal featured on the cover of *Programming with curses* is a babirusa or Celebes pig deer. This wild pig inhabits the jungles and woodlands of Celebes and neighbouring islands in the Malay Archipelago. 27 inches in height, the babirusa has wrinkled grey skin which falls in folds over its head, shoulders and neck. It has practically no hair, and its legs are unusually long for a pig.

The babirusa is easily identified by its tusks; upper canines which grow throughout its lifetime, frequently reaching lengths of 17 inches. These tusks curl upward and backward, sometimes reaching the forehead. Though distinctive, these tusks appear to have no use. Indeed, they may be a hinderance, for, though the babirusa feeds on shellfish, herbs and grasses, it does not root about in the soil for food like most pigs.

Edie Freedman designed this cover and the entire UNIX bestiary that appears on other Nutshell Handbooks. The beasts themselves are adapted from 19th-century engravings from the Dover Pictorial Archive.

The text of this book is set in Times Roman; headings are Helvetica; examples are Courier. Text was prepared using SoftQuad's sqtroff text formatter. Printing is done on an Apple LaserWriter.